A MEDITATION THEME FOR EACH DAY

From the teachings of
Hazrat Inayat Khan

Selected, edited and arranged
by Pir Vilayat Khan

OMEGA PUBLICATIONS
New Lebanon

A Meditation Theme for Each Day
New editiion published July, 1992

OMEGA PUBLICATIONS INC
RD 1 Box 1030E
New Lebanon NY 12125

Printed in the U.S.A.
ISBN 0-930872-45-2
10 9 8 7 6 5 4 3 2 1

These themes for one's daily meditation have been drawn from the comprehensive teaching of a Sufi master. Topics are developed over several days and weeks, supporting depth in spiritual practice, and over the course of the year the breadth of an authentic spiritual viewpoint unfolds.

Slight revisions and corrections have been made to the text as it appeared in the 1982 edition. The primary resource in making these changes has been *The Message in our Time*, Pir Vilayat Khan's biographical study of Pir-o-Murshid Inayat Khan, in which many of the same themes are considered in a broader context.

— The Publisher

January 1

With the maturity of his soul, a man desires to probe the depths of life, he desires to discover the power latent within him, he longs to know the sources and goal of his life, he yearns to understand the aim and meaning of his life, he wishes to understand the inner significance of things, and he wants to uncover all that is covered by name and form. He seeks for insight into cause and effect, he wants to touch the mystery of time and space, and he wishes to find the missing link between God and man — where man ends, where God begins.

January 2

In the beginning when there was no earth, no heaven, there was no other plane of existence than eternal awareness which may be called a silent, inactive state of life, or unawakened intelligence, that men have idealized as God, the only Being. Within it, there awakened of its own nature the awareness of its own existence, unlimited by knowledge of form and space.

January 3

The whole of creation was made in order to awaken. But awakening is chiefly of two kinds: one kind is called birth, the birth of the body when the soul awakens in a condition where it is limited in the physical body, and so man becomes captive; and there is another awakening, which is to awaken to reality, and that is called the birth of the soul. God lost in manifestation is the state that we call awakening. Manifestation lost in God is realization. In my language I would call the former dream and the latter awakening.

January 4

Every atom, every object, every condition, and every living being has a time of awakening. Sometimes this is a gradual awakening and sometimes it is sudden. To some people it comes in a moment's time by some blow or disappointment, or because their heart has been broken through something that happened suddenly.

January 5

We live in the world to which we are awakened, and to the world to which we are not awakened we are asleep. We are asleep to that part of life which we do not know. What is the sign that one is ready to awaken from sleep? It is when a person begins to think, "All that I have learned and understood

seems so unreal; there are some realities of which I
am vaguely aware, and yet compared with them all I
have studied and done seems to be of no account."

January 6

It is not our usual experience to wake up suddenly
one day from sleep and find that our point of view
has changed, but it is no exaggeration to say that it
takes but one moment to change one's outlook on
life entirely. Spiritual progress is the changing of the
point of view. This is what initiation is. We go on in
life from one initiation to the next, and each step on
the ladder that seems to be standing before us for us
to climb becomes an initiation. And each step on
that ladder changes our point of view if only we
hold on to the ladder and do not drop down: for
there is always the possibility of going either
forward or backward.

January 7

What at one time gives man great satisfaction at
another time humiliates him.

January 8

It is the awakening of the soul which is mentioned
in the Bible: unless the soul is born again it will not
enter the kingdom of heaven. For the soul to be
born again means that it is awakened after having
come on earth, and entering the kingdom of heaven
means entering this world in which we are now

standing, the same kingdom which turns into
heaven as soon as the point of view has changed. Is
it not interesting and most wonderful to think that
the same earth that we walk on is earth to one
person and heaven to another? And it is still more
interesting to notice that it is we who change it from
earth to heaven. This change comes not by study
nor by anything else but by the changing of our
point of view.

January 9

When the soul is awakened, it is as if that person
were to wake up in the middle of the night among
hundreds and thousands of people who were fast
asleep. He is sitting or standing among them,
hearing about their sorrows and miseries and their
conditions, hundreds of them moving about in their
sleep, in their dreams, not awakened to his
condition although he is near them. They know
little about him, as each one is absorbed in his own
trouble. This awakened soul, standing among them
all, will listen to everyone, will recognize all that
they think and feel; but his language no one
understands; his thoughts he cannot explain to
anyone; his feelings he cannot expect anyone to feel.
He feels lonely, but no doubt in this loneliness there
is also the sense of perfection, for perfection is
always lonely. Imagine living in a world where
nobody speaks our language. Yet he knows the
world's language. The experience of the matured
soul is like the experience of the man who watched a
play performed on stage at night, and in the

morning he saw the same stage again in the sun and saw that all the palaces and gardens and the actors' costumes were unreal.

January 10

Things that seem real to an average person are unreal in the eyes of the mystic, and the things that seem unreal in the eyes of the average person are real in the eyes of the mystic. Little things that people take to heart will seem to him of little importance; things that people become confused with will become clear to him; things that matter so much to everyone will not matter to him; many things that frighten and horrify people will not have the same effect upon him; disappointments and failures will not take away his hope and courage. His thought, speech and action change: as his outlook becomes wide, so everything he says or does will be different. In the first place mystical life is a puzzle, in the second place a bewilderment, and in the third place a miracle. There comes a time when all that he had accepted in his mind, all that he believed in, appears to be quite the contrary to what it seemed before: his friends, his relations, those whom he loved, everything. Wealth, position, all the things he has pursued, all change their appearance and sometimes seem to become quite the opposite of what they seemed. Imagine an evolved person being more bewildered than an unevolved one. And yet it is so, for at this stage a man begins to see that things are not as they seem.

January 11

The first sign one notices after the awakening of the soul is that one begins to see from two points of view. One begins to see the right of the wrong and the wrong of the right. In failure one will not feel such disappointment, and in success not such a great joy. In adverse conditions one will not be so dejected, in favorable conditions not so conceited. One begins to see that everything is reflected in its opposite. In this way one rises above logic, which then begins to appear as an elementary knowledge. It is a kind of double view of things. And when one has reached this, then reason has made way for higher reasoning. No doubt one's language will become gibberish to others; people will not understand it. To some it will be too simple, to others too subtle.

January 12

Every thought that has once crossed the mind, every feeling that has once passed through the heart, every word that is once spoken and perhaps never thought about any longer, every action once done and forgotten, is given a life, and it continues to live. It is just like a traveller who is journeying, and on his way he has some seeds in his hands and throws them on the ground. When the plants grow in that place he never sees them; he just threw the seeds and they are there.

January 13

Everything that is once felt, thought, or spoken is born as a living being, with a destiny, with a purpose to fulfill; and as it has birth, it necessarily has death. Therefore, besides living beings, feelings, words, thoughts, and the effects of one's actions float in the air, rise up and come down, swing hither and thither, and seek their location in objects and in living beings.

January 14

Thoughts are beings. They are as much living beings as we are.

January 15

You must ever bear in mind that the light and life that go out from you to the object are quite as important as that light that comes to you from the object. Thought is activity of the consciousness impressed by the external world.

January 16

There is a knowledge that one can perceive with the senses, and there is a knowledge that one can perceive with the mind alone, and a knowledge that can be realized by the soul.

January 17

Man experiences heaven when conscious of his soul;
he experiences the earth when conscious of his
body. Man experiences that plane which is between
heaven and earth when he is conscious of his mind.

January 18

The soul produces the mind out of its own self, and
yet the mind is constructed fully after the formation
of the body. The experience the mind gains through
the body as its vehicle becomes its knowledge, and it
is knowledge that makes mind. What in the soul
may be called vibration, in the body becomes atom.
The physical body becomes dependent in its
experience and expression, thus making the soul
dependent and limited. If the soul could see
independently of the mind and body, it would see
infinitely more.

January 19

The soul is like a light in the room that is the mind,
for the soul perceives feeling, thought, memory,
reason, and identity, and identifies itself with them.
In reality it is aloof from them. But as the soul
cannot see itself, it thinks, with the help of the ego,
"I am sad," or, "I am glad," or, "I remember," or, "I
have forgotten." In reality the soul does none of
these things; they are all the workings of the mind,
but it identifies itself with what it sees at this time.

January 20

After death, that which the soul had known as mind, that very mind is now to the soul a world; that which the soul while on earth called imagination is now before it a reality. In this world our mind is in us. In the next world we are in our mind.

January 21

There is a still deeper sphere to which our memory is linked, and that sphere is the universal memory, in other words, the divine mind.

January 22

We recognize intelligence in its manifestation, but we do not know it in its essence.

January 23

Consciousness must always be conscious of something. When consciousness is not conscious of anything, it is pure intelligence.

January 24

There is a difference between intelligence and something that is intelligent. Intelligence in which a certain consciousness is reflected becomes intelligent, but intelligence need not know, in the same way that consciousness need not be conscious of anything; it is the knowing faculty.

January 25

Intelligence confined to knowledge of phenomena becomes limited, but when it is free from all knowledge then it experiences its own essence.

January 26

It is the consciousness itself that has involved a part of itself in its creation, while a part remains as Creator, as water frozen turns into ice and yet water abides within.

January 27

All that one sees during the day and night is not what one intended to see, but what one is compelled by the life around one to see.

January 28

Everything in life is speaking, is audible, is communicating, in spite of its apparent silence.

January 29

Insight is the opening of the sight to a higher plane of one's being. Why a person does not observe the unseen world is that he is accustomed to observe only what is before him.

January 30

Turn the eyes back, turn the eyes within. Then the same eyes that are able to see without are able to see within. Sometimes the third eye sees through the two eyes, and then the same eyes see things more clearly than they would otherwise.

January 31

The eyes are given to see; the soul to see further.

February 1

The mystics, the Sufis, have ways of developing the eyes. They show you ways of looking into space that make the eyes capable of seeing what is reflected there. From these reflections the past, present, and future can be told, and all that surrounds a person.

February 2

The awakened person throws light, the light of his soul, upon every creature and every object, and sees that object, person, or condition in this light.

February 3

Sometimes innocent people have a better understanding of a person than clever people with deceitful minds.

February 4

The feelings of another can tell you much more than his words and actions can.

February 5

How often when people are in close touch do they perceive each other's condition not only by thought waves, but in the realm of feeling also. This shows that there is one body, and that in that body there is one life which continually circulates, as the blood does in our veins.

February 6

It is by seeing the cause of every fault in oneself that one is able to have insight into human nature.

February 7

It is disclosure of one's own spirit that unveils all things.

February 8

It is the seer's own soul that becomes a torch in his hand; it is his own light that illuminates his path. It is just like directing a searchlight into dark corners which one could not see before so that the corners become clear and illuminated. It is like throwing light upon problems that one did not understand before, like seeing through people with x-rays when they were a riddle before. He who looks at this marvel begins to see the divine evidence in every face, as a person can see the painter in his painting.

February 9

There is a stage of evolution in one's life when one arrives at a state when every question is answered by the life around him. The answer to his question comes as the re-echo of the very question. For every thought of a sage, everything becomes an accommodation to help it to resound, and in this resonance there is an answer. In point of fact the answer is in the question itself. The answer wells up from the depth of all existence, like the sound of a bell being struck, or the splash of water, or the crackle of the firecracker: each reveals its condition when struck, like the knock on the door.

February 10

For the mystic, everything is connected: there is no condition that is detached from another condition. A mechanism is always running in relation to another mechanism, however different and disconnected they may seem. To gain insight into things the mystic enters into the depths of the whole mechanism of the universe.

February 11

The eye of the seer becomes like a sword that cuts open, so to speak, all things, including the hearts of men, and sees clearly all they contain. This glance opens, unlocks, and unfolds things. It is not actually creating, but it is awakening that particular quality which was perhaps asleep.

February 12

The seer's discerning of the condition of those before him and away from him is likened to the process of eating and digesting. The mouth distinguishes between sweet and sour, vegetable and cereal, but once food is swallowed, then what is felt about it is the feeling, not the outer distinctions but the inner essence. Therefore the seer re-analyzes something which the person whom he sees has analyzed with his mind. He becomes one with another person, experiencing what his mind has experienced, and likewise with his soul.

February 13

The person whose glance is like an x-ray sees through a person. This person will find more faults, lacks, wants in human nature, but it is this person who will be less affected by them or overlook them and rise above them. The reason is that he sees the cause, and when he sees the cause he sees the effect.

February 14

To the seer every person's soul is just like an open letter, but if he were to divulge its secrets his sight would become dimmer every day, because it is a trust given to him by God. Spiritual trust is given to those who can keep that trust and who are able to keep a secret.

February 15

The poet when he is developed reads the mind of the universe, although it very often happens that the poet himself does not know the real meaning of what he has said.

February 16

The one who tunes himself not only to the external but to the inner being and to the essence of all things gets an insight into the essence of the whole being, and therefore he can to the same extent find and enjoy even in the seed the fragrance and beauty which delight him in a rose. He, so to speak, touches the soul of the thought. It is just as by seeing the plant one may get an idea of the root. And in this way things unknown are known and things unseen are perceived by the mystic, and he calls it revelation.

February 17

Intuition can be described as a glimpse of knowledge that one has stored within oneself, that comes at a time when it is needed. It is a disclosure of one's own spirit that unveils all things. It is by seeing the cause of every fault in oneself that one is able to have insight into human nature.

February 18

In order to make the intuition clear, the best thing is to stop the imagination.

February 19

Every imagination is intuition until it has been corrupted by reason, and when the intuition is corrupted by reason it becomes fantasy. For as soon as we begin to think it out, we at once descend from the higher, the spiritual source of information, and use earthly means to establish what belongs to heaven. Therefore the first condition is to separate this outer knowledge from the inner knowing.

February 20

It is quite possible for the thought of another person to float into that field of which one is conscious, and one may hear it and think it is one's intuition.

February 21

We ought to build a fence around intuitions as if they were delicate plants.

February 22

In the physical world, you are here and everything else is without you. You are contained in space. In the dream, all that you see is contained within you.

February 23

If all that we see in dreams is we ourselves, then why do we see ourselves even in dreams as an identity separate from all other things before us in the dream? The answer is, "Because the soul is deluded by our external form, and it recognizes this picture as 'I'. All other images and forms manifesting before it in the dream stand in contrast to this 'I'."

February 24

In an astral vision a relation or a friend may appear to a person and tell him something about the other side of life. Before another a saint or sage may appear. One may see the vision of one's friends or relations, past and present. One may see faces never seen before, and yet faces that once existed in the world. When the visions are clear it is the moment when the soul is clear from all earthly shadows, and therefore heavenly pictures, so to speak, appear upon the curtain of man's heart. Every unseen form that we see in a vision, be it of a spirit, fairy, or angel, or of a teacher, sage, or saint, is according to man's evolution. As highly evolved a person is, so high is his vision. Sometimes he attracts the object of his vision, sometimes the object of his vision wishes to manifest to him, and sometimes he creates the object of his vision before him.

February 25

There are two views of life, which represent two different temperaments, and which may be compared to short sight and long sight, to the view at short range and the view at long range. The former notices in detail and sees closely into the facts of material life, and the latter touches the furthest horizon.

February 26

Look up first, and when your eyes are once charged with divine light, then when you cast your glance on the world of facts you will have a much clearer vision, the vision of reality.

February 27

In order to attain to inner knowledge the Sufi covers the other side of the soul, so that its mirror part may face the spirit instead of the outer world. As soon as he is able to accomplish this he receives inspirations and revelations.

February 28

Those who dive deep within themselves can, when they touch the plane of the abstract, perceive things that are preparing to manifest through the mind onto the surface. But the primitive state of these things is so indistinct even to the seer that unless he

knows the language of that sphere he cannot
understand what his experiences convey.

February 29

For everything there is an appointed time, and
when that time comes, revelation comes.

March 1

As one goes further in the soul's unfoldment one finally arrives at the stage of revelation. Life begins to reveal itself, and every condition, every soul, every object in the world will reveal its nature and character to one.

March 2

For us limited beings to say that this world has no reality seems a blasphemy. It is all right for us to feel this, but it is not right to say it, because if you are to say it, you must prove it by your independence of this illusion. A claim that has not yet been put into practice is not a good claim. That is why a mystic will always refrain from saying such a thing as that all this is an illusion. But he tries to feel it more and more every day.

March 3

Illusion is the cover of things; reality is the depth of things.

March 4

A child must be taught from the beginning that
things are not as he sees just now, but that when he
sees differently he will find the same thing different.

March 5

As man evolves he naturally ceases to look down on
earth, but looks up to the cosmos, the heavens. So if
one wants to seek heaven, one must change the
direction of looking.

March 6

Not all the knowledge learned from books and from
experiences in the world and collected in the mind
as learning is wisdom. When the light from within is
thrown upon this knowledge, then the knowledge
from outer life and the light coming from within
make perfect wisdom; and it is that wisdom that
guides man on the path of life.

March 7

When a person awakens to the spirit of unity and
sees the oneness behind all things, his point of view
becomes different, and his attitude changes thereby.
There is nothing and no one who is divided or
separate from him, so he experiences everything as
the self of each being. When the consciousness of
the external self is gone, then whatever appears
before him is his self.

March 8

I first believed without any hesitation in the existence of the soul, and then I wondered about the secret of its nature. I persevered and strove in search of the soul, and found at last that I myself was the cover over my own soul. I realized that that in me which believed and that in me which wondered, that which was found at last, was no other than my soul. I thanked the darkness that brought me to the light, and I valued this veil that prepared for me the vision in which I saw myself reflected, the vision produced in the mirror of my soul. Since then I have seen all souls as my soul, and realized my soul as the soul of all. And what bewilderment it was when I realized that I alone was, if there were anyone; that I am whatever and whoever exists; and that I shall be whoever there will be in the future. And there was no end to my happiness and joy. Verily, I am the seed and I am the root, and I am the fruit of this tree of life.

March 9

It is to gather knowledge that the soul has come on earth. Looking into the past is just like looking deep down from great heights. It means probing the depths of life. Looking into the present is just like observing a wide horizon, as wide as we can see. Looking into the future is like looking upward to the zenith. In self-knowledge of past and present and future one has to learn what was the origin of

the soul, how the soul has formed itself, how it has
come to manifest, the knowledge of the process of
manifestation, and the different stages through
which it has passed towards manifestation.
Regarding the present one should learn one's own
condition, the condition of one's spirit, of one's
mind and body, one's situation in life, and one's
individual relationship to others. One should also
realize how far the soul reaches in the spiritual
spheres.

March 10

The soul is an individuated portion of the
all-pervading consciousness. It is undivided because
it is the absolute Being; it is completely filled with
the whole existence. The portion of it that is
reflected by a certain name or form becomes
comparatively more conscious of the object reflected
in it than of all other objects. Our minds and bodies,
being reflected upon a portion of the all-pervading
consciousness, make that part of consciousness an
all-pervading soul which in reality is a universal
spirit. The soul in itself alone is no other than
consciousness, which is all-pervading. But when the
same consciousness is caught in a limitation through
being surrounded by elements, in that state of
captivity it is called the soul.

March 11

At the cost of the happiness of heaven, the soul
comes to the great fulfillment of life, which even

angels are not blessed with; for manifestation in human form is the utmost boundary of manifestation, the furthest that any soul can go.

March 12

Those who think that the heavenly knowledge is sufficient are mystical, but the joy of the heavenly knowledge and the full understanding of it come from being able to express it in this world's medium of expression.

March 13

Every soul starts toward manifestation with the inclination of arriving at the destination of his journey, and that destination is the human plane. While descending toward this destination, every soul touches two distinct planes on its way, the angelic and the djinn plane. There are souls who, owing to lack of strength or owing to the attraction of a certain plane, remain and settle in that plane, instead of progressing further. But there are some who come to their real destination, and it is they who fulfil the purpose of life. It is therefore that man is considered greater than the djinn and higher than the angel.

March 14

There are some souls who halt in their journey to earth at either the djinn or the angelic plane a much longer time than a traveling soul would usually stay.

And yet they cannot stay: the energy that is still
there keeps them restless until they have
accomplished their journey. Therefore, they come on
earth as human beings, yet showing in their nature
the character of the plane at which they had
stationed on their way. They cannot help feeling
homesick, for they often unconsciously feel that
they do not belong to this earth, that they had some
experience somewhere else that they long to have
again. And the only way these souls can find is
through the love of art, science, or knowledge to the
djinn world, and through piety, purity, and
spirituality to the angelic plane. This not only gives
them a substitute for the life they have had, but to a
greater or less extent the realization of that plane,
because in the human being all planes are manifest.

March 15

The nature of the soul is to gather on its way all that
it can gather and to make a mold out of it. The
attributes of the lower world become so clustered
around the soul that it almost forgets its very first
experience of itself, its purest being. In the angelic
sphere the soul attracts angelic atoms, in the djinn
sphere it attracts djinn atoms, and on earth, physical
atoms, Thus mankind is clothed in the garb of an
angel, of a djinn, and of a human being. But when
he sees himself in the garb of a human being
without seeing the other garbs, he believes he is a
human being.

March 16

Apart from inheriting qualities that belong to its parents and ancestors, the soul picks up the reflection that it has brought with it before it came to this physical plane. Consciously or unconsciously we call to us that element which makes us what we are. What we experience in life, therefore, has either come from what we have already called to us in the past or from what we call at the present moment.

March 17

The soul acquires only those qualities in which it is interested, and the soul keeps only those attributes in which it is interested. However many undesirable attributes a person may have, he can lose them all if he does not approve of them.

March 18

Does the soul consciously and intentionally chose its parents? Yes, according to its consciousness at that time.

March 19

It is the direction of the activity of vibrations that accounts for the variety of things and beings. It is a certain degree of vibration that brings to the earth the things of the inner world, and a change of vibrations takes away the things that are seen into the unseen world.

March 20

The next world is the same as this, and this world is the same as the next, only what is veiled from our eyes we call the unseen world. And the reason why a person does not observe the unseen world is that he is accustomed to observe only what is before him; he never turns within to see what is within him.

March 21

"In the other world" means in a world which is veiled from our eyes, our physical eyes; but it does not mean a world far away from us, beyond our reach. Both the living and the dead inhabit the same space; we all live together. Only a veil separates us, the veil of this physical body. Separation means being unable to see one another. There is no other separation.

March 22

The mind is a world, a world that man makes and in which he will make his life in the hereafter, as a spider lives in the web it has woven.

March 23

There are three principle components: one, the heritage of the soul that it has brought from the angelic world and from the djinn world: second, the inherited qualities that a soul possesses, having received them from its parents and ancestors; and

third, what the soul acquires after coming on earth.
It is these three things that make what can be called
individuality, which, in its result, culminates in a
personality.

March 24

Every child born on earth possesses, besides that
which he has inherited from his parents and
ancestors, a power and knowledge quite peculiar to
himself and different from that which his parents
and ancestors possessed.

March 25

No doubt the soul who has passed from earth
returns the same way: passing through the plane of
the djinn, it arrives in the world of angels. And in
that way a person who has passed recovers his inner
being as a djinn or an angel. And yet he is not the
same as the beings belonging to that plane, because
he goes with the additional knowledge that he has
gained in the earthly plane.

March 26

The souls coming out get impressions from souls
going back because they absorb, conceive, learn, and
receive all that is given to them by the souls leaving
the earth.

March 27

In the fountain there are two kinds of drops: the one constantly touches the source and goal; the other rises, breaks on the way, and so drops in the source disconnected on the way. The latter is the life of the people who simply live and die.

March 28

When the soul comes into the physical world it receives an offering from the whole universe, and that offering is the body in which to function. It is not offered to the soul only by the parents, but by the ancestors, by the nation and race into which the soul is born, and by the whole human race. This body is not only an offering of the human race, but is an outcome of something that the whole world has produced for ages, a clay that has been kneaded a thousand times over, a clay that has been prepared so that in its very development it has become more intelligent, more radiant, and more living; a clay that appeared first in the mineral kingdom, that developed in the vegetable kingdom, that then appeared as the animal, and that was finished in the making of that body that is offered to the new-coming human soul.

March 29

In the depth of the soul there is the quality that it has brought with it; on the surface is the quality that the ancestors have given it. If that innate quality is greater, then it may also manifest on the surface, covering that quality that the parents and ancestors have given it. Another way of a soul's inheriting qualities that do not belong to its parents and ancestors is the reflection that a soul has brought with it before it has come to this physical plane. There is also the inheritance from the minds of those who have left this earth. When a soul on its way to the earth meets a soul coming from this world, it receives the impressions of that soul.

March 30

On its return journey the soul gives back all its properties to their own sources. Then it is the soul in its own essence that is left, merging into the ocean of consciousness where nothing of its previous properties remains. Even its love and kindness and its nice feelings it cannot take higher than the world of the angels.

March 31

While on earth paradise is an imagination, in the hereafter the same paradise will become a reality.

April 1

The Sufi believes that consciousness has, so to speak, produced matter, or substance, out of itself, while yet remaining itself in its original state.

April 2

If matter did not have spirit in it, it would not awaken.

April 3

The soul manifesting as a body has diminished its power considerably, even to the extent that it is not capable of imagining for one moment the great power, life, and light it has in itself. Once the soul realizes itself by becoming independent of the body that surrounds it, the soul naturally begins to see in itself the being of the spirit.

April 4

Once a person has realized how he can exist without the physical body, it produces a faith that gives an ultimate conviction which nothing can change.

April 5

He who knows spirit receives far greater inspiration from being able to exist independently of the physical body.

April 6

All that lives is spirit, and all that dies is matter.

April 7

To whom the soul truly belongs, to Him in the end it returns.

April 8

As soon as a person is able to look at his spirit he is born again. By looking at one's spirit one can analyze how all that one says, thinks, and feels acts upon one's spirit, and also how the spirit reacts.

April 9

To keep the spirit in proper condition is as difficult as or even more difficult than cultivating a delicate plant in a greenhouse, where a little more sun may spoil it, a little more water may destroy it, a little more wind may be bad for it. The spirit is even more delicate than that. A slight shadow of deception, a mere feeling of dishonesty, a little touch of

shakes it, if anger strikes deep into its root, it is
spoiled. A slight sense of dishonor, the least insult
coming from any side can kill it. The mystic
therefore trains his spirit. It is the training of his
own spirit that enables a man to help the souls who
come to him.

April 10

We want a human spirit, and self-realization is the
search for this human spirit.

April 11

One can read in the lives of great heroes and great
personalities how they went through all difficulties
and sorrows and troubles, and yet always tried to
keep their hearts from being humiliated.

April 12

It is better that a person should die than that his
spirit should.

April 13

We are as great as our spirit, we are as wide as our
spirit, we are as low as our spirit, we are as small as
our spirit; spirit can make us all that we are.

April 14

Success or failure, happiness or unhappiness, all
depend upon the condition of the spirit.

April 15

The flame of a match cannot stand up to the wind. Therefore it is the weak-spirited ones who can fret about their life's conditions and fall because their spirit lacks strength and power.

April 16

Not everyone can raise his spirit when once it is fallen, for then it is heavier to lift than a mountain.

April 17

The spirit distinguishes everything except itself, just as the eyes cannot see themselves.

April 18

If it is the very same spirit that we breathe from space that makes man capable of thinking and feeling, the same spirit that gives him the power of perception and conception and develops in him that feeling that one calls ego, if this is the phenomenon that the spirit shows by being absorbed by the material body, how much more capable of perception and conception, of thought and feeling, must the spirit be in itself.

April 19

The phrase "to pull oneself together" means to set that part of life to work which may be called spirit.

April 20

In reality matter comes from spirit; matter in its true nature is spirit; matter is an action of spirit that has materialized and has become a reality to our senses, hiding the spirit under it. It has covered the existence of the spirit from the eyes of those who look at life from the outside.

April 21

The qualities of all things are to be found in their spirit rather than in the things themselves.

April 22

The difference between spirit and matter is like the difference between water and ice: frozen water is ice, and melted ice is water. It is spirit in its denseness that we call matter; it is matter in its fineness that may be called spirit. If there is water and ice, the water will run, the ice will stay where it is. It does not mean that ice will not return to its original condition: it will, but its time has not yet come.

April 23

There is a conflict between spirit and matter. Matter absorbs the spirit in order to exist, and the spirit assimilates matter, for it is its own property. The whole of manifestation may thus be regarded as a continual conflict between spirit and matter, the spirit developing into matter on the one hand and assimilating matter on the other: the former being called activity and the latter silence, or construction and destruction, or life and death.

April 24

All that is constructed is subject to destruction; all that is composed must be decomposed; all that is formed must be destroyed; that which has birth has death. But all this belongs to matter: the spirit that is absorbed by this formation of matter or by its mechanism lives, for spirit cannot die. What we call life is an absorption of spirit by matter. As long as the matter is strong and energetic enough to absorb life or spirit from space, it continues to live and move and be in good condition, but when it has lost its grip on the spirit, when it cannot absorb the spirit as it ought to, then it cannot live, for the substance of matter is spirit.

April 25

Two waves are a temporary condition of the water of the sea. The water of the sea remains; it is only a temporary condition of the rising of the water that makes a space between two waves. They are and they are not.

April 26

As long as the spirit is interested in the physical body it holds it, permeates it, and embraces it. But as soon as it feels that it no longer has any use for the body, it drops it.

April 27

It is the strength of the physical body that holds the spirit, and it is the strength of the spirit that holds the body.

April 28

The law of gravitation is only half known to the world of science, which believes that the earth attracts all that belongs to it. This is true. But the spirit also attracts all that belongs to it, and that other side to the law of gravitation has always been known to the mystics.

April 29

There are four different explanations of the word spirit. One meaning is essence. The second meaning of spirit is what is understood by those who call the soul spirit when it has left the body on earth and has passed to the other side. The third meaning is that of the soul and mind working together. It is used in this sense when one says that a man seems to be in low spirits. And the fourth meaning of spirit is the soul of all souls, the source and goal of all things and all beings, from which all comes and to which all returns.

April 30

Spirit is not a very appropriate word for the soul that has passed from the physical plane. Really speaking, there is only one spirit, the spirit of all, the rays of which are all souls.

May 1

If we say that there are many souls, it is true, just as there are many waves or many rays of the sun; but if we say there is one spirit, it is truer still, just as there is one sea and one sun. The waves are an action of the sea, the rays are a manifestation of the sun, the souls are a phenomenon of the spirit. They are and they are not. They are because we see them, and they are not because there is only one Being.

May 2

Some people will call spirit energy, or a scientist will give it the name of some form or force, but it is never called a person or a being.

May 3

Spirit is matter, and matter is spirit. The denseness of spirit is matter, and the fineness of matter is spirit.

May 4

All souls, by the right and the wrong path, either sooner or later, will arrive at that purpose which must be accomplished, a purpose for which the whole creation has been intended.

May 5

No one will experience in life what is not meant for him.

May 6

There is nothing in this world without a purpose, and, though the place of one in the scheme of life may seem different from that of another, yet in the total of things we and the lower creation, together with the djinn and angels, have our purpose. That purpose is the realization of truth.

May 7

The clay works toward the purpose of forming a vessel and so does the potter, but it is the potter's joy and privilege to feel the happiness of the accomplishment of the purpose, not the clay's.

May 8

The seed comes last, after the life of trunk, branch, fruit, and flower, and as the seed is sufficient in itself and capable of producing another plant, so man is the product of all the planes, spiritual and material, and yet in him alone shines forth that primal intelligence that caused the whole, the seed of existence: God.

May 9

Divinity is like the seed that grows in the heart of the flower: it is the same seed that was the origin of the plant, and it comes again in the heart of the flower. In a similar way the same God who was unmanifested as the seed of the plant of this creation rises again towards fulfillment, and in that fulfillment He produces the seed in the heart of that flower which is divinity.

May 10

The effect is in the cause and the cause is in the effect, as the flower is the outcome of the seed and the seed is in the heart of the flower.

May 11

The purpose seems to be in the cause, but it is finished in the effect.

May 12

To understand cause and effect is to be able to find the cause of the cause and the effect of the effect.

May 13

There is not always the same process, because God is not subject to law and His creation not subject to a process. And the habit He makes in one creation is called nature, and those who perceive its process recognize the process of the change of nature, His law. This law does not hold good in every cycle of creation, though it is significant to some extent in that particular cycle of creation. And those who have insight into that law are called seers.

May 14

In matter life unfolds, discovers, and realizes the consciousness that has been, so to speak, buried in it for thousands of years.

May 15

The conception that the physical body is made of sin and that this is the lowest aspect of being will very often prove to be a mistake, for it is through the physical body that the highest and the greatest purpose of life is to be achieved.

May 16

The purpose of life is like the horizon: the further one advances, the further it recedes.

May 17

There is a pair of opposites in all things; in each thing there exists the spirit of the opposite.

May 18

The whole of creation was a process to make that image which was the image of man.

May 19

It is not by self-realization that man realizes God, it is by God-realization that man realizes self.

May 20

My thoughts I have sown on the soil of your mind; My love has penetrated your heart; My word I have put into your mouth; My light has illuminated your whole being; My work I have put into your hand.

May 21

When Though didst sit upon Thy throne, with a crown upon Thy head, I did prostrate myself upon the ground and called Thee my lord.

When Thou didst stretch out Thy hands in blessing over me, I knelt and called Thee my master.

When Thou didst raise me from the ground, holding me with Thine arms, I drew closer to Thee and called Thee my beloved.

But when Thy caressing hands held my head next to Thy glowing heart and Thou didst kiss me, I smiled and called Thee myself.

May 22

Deity is God idealized and divinity is God personified. The whole difficulty that has occurred in all periods of the world's history has been the difficulty of understanding divinity or apprehending the mystery of divinity. Man cannot think of man being God, nor can man think of God being man. Therefore the claimant of divinity has been brought to earth and called no better than man. Deity is the enshrined God whom man has conceived by his thoughts and ideas; in that way the ideas about deity came to differ. Therefore the deity of every heart is different, and is as that person has imagined; but the God of every soul is one and the same, whatever people imagine. And it is the lack of understanding of this that has caused the differences in religion.

May 23

Some religious authorities have tried to recognize the divinity of Christ while ignoring the divinity of humanity. They have tried to make Christ different from what may be called human; but by doing so they have covered the main truth that religion had to give to the world, which was that divinity resides in humanity, that divinity is the outcome of humanity, and that humanity is the flower in the heart of which divinity was born as a seed. It is the development of humanity that culminates in divinity; thus Christ is the example of the culmination of humanity. It would be hiding the greatest human virtue to hide this secret, which is the key to the mystery of the whole universe.

May 24

God always comes and always shows Himself through the heart of the godly. The comparison of the divine with God is just like a sunglass placed before the sun. The sunglass partakes of the heat of the sun and transfers the heat to the earth; and so the divine man, the messenger in all ages, comes and partakes of God's rays and hands them down to earth in the form of the divine message. Although a sunglass is not the sun, yet when it is exposed to the sun it partakes of the sun and begins to show the quality of the sun. So it is with the souls who focus their hearts on God. And then all that is in God becomes manifest in man.

May 25

Man's grade of evolution depends upon the pitch he has attained; it is a certain pitch that makes him conscious of a certain phase of life. A man who is standing upon the earth and is talking about the air does not know what is in the air. He must rise to where the air is and then he must get the experience and talk from there about what he is experiencing. It is not by theory that a person can trace his origin. He can only do so by practice. It is not only knowing a thing, but living it and being it.

May 26

The Creator takes the heart of man through which to experience the whole of creation. It is through man that God contemplates His creation.

May 27

He creates of Himself. Therefore the creation and the Creator are not two, or rather, they are two but at the same time they are not.

May 28

In man is awakened that spirit by which the whole universe was created.

May 29

The work of the inner life is to make God a reality, so that He is no more an imagination, that this relationship that man has with God may seem to him more real than any other relationship in this world.

May 30

In reality He feels what we imagine we feel, yet at the same time His perfect being keeps Him above all earthly joys and pains.

May 31

True exaltation of the spirit resides in the fact that it has come to earth and has realized there its spiritual existence.

June 1

How is higher consciousness attained? By closing our eyes to our limited self and by opening our heart to the God who is all perfection, who is in heaven and on earth and who is within and without, the God who is all in all, who is visible, tangible, audible, perceptible, intelligible, and yet beyond man's comprehension.

June 2

That active part of the consciousness that has produced the whole manifestation cannot be compared to the eternal consciousness.

June 3

In creation God Himself manifests. In suffering He Himself suffers; He Himself is puzzled in His creation: and one day He Himself realizes His perfection. God only exists, no one else.

June 4

Manifestation is the self of God, but a self that is
limited, a self that makes Him know that He is
perfect when He compares His own being with this
limited self that we call nature. Therefore the
purpose of the whole of creation is the realization
that God Himself gains by discovering His own
perfection through this manifestation. The purpose
of life, in short, is that the Only Being makes His
oneness intelligible to Himself. He goes through
different planes of evolution, or planes through
which He arrives at different changes, in order to
make clear to Himself His oneness. And as long as
this purpose is not accomplished, the One and Only
Being has not reached His ultimate satisfaction, in
which lies His divine perfection.

June 5

The fulfillment of this whole creation is to be found
in man. And this object is only fulfilled when man
has awakened to that part of his being which
represents the master: in other words, God Himself.
It is in man that the divine perfection is to be seen.
He identified himself with that spirit of which he
was conscious, with that spirit of perfection which
lived before Jesus, and will continue to live till the
end of the world, of eternity.

June 6

The rasul is the soul through which God Himself has attained that which is the purpose of creation; in other words, the rasul is the one who represents God's perfection through human limitation. Divinity is the outcome of humanity.

June 7

God is human perfection, and man is divine limitation.

June 8

One who is conscious of his earthly origin is an earthly man; one who is conscious of his heavenly origin is the son of God. He is a son of man who has recognized himself as the son of his parents, who are as limited as he. It seems as if the knowledge of his own being is buried within himself.

June 9

There cannot exist two beings, God and oneself. Oneself, as one knows the self, is a limited part of being, like a bubble in the sea that has no existence of its own. It is only a temporary condition. By effacing oneself one does not annihilate oneself: it is the finding of the self, a self that is perfect.

June 10

How can the unlimited Being be limited, since all
that seems limited is, in its depth, beyond all
limitation?

June 11

If the planet is an ocean, then the individual is a
drop. But inwardly the planet is a drop in the ocean
of man.

June 12

The nature of being in tune with the infinite is this:
comparing our soul to a string of an instrument, it is
tied at both ends; one is the infinite, and the other is
the finite. When a person is conscious all the time of
the finite then he is tuned to the finite, while the
one who is conscious of the infinite is tuned to the
infinite. Being in tune with the former makes us
limited, weak, hopeless, and powerless; but by being
in tune with the latter we obtain the power and
strength that will pull us through life in whatever
adverse conditions may arise.

June 13

What is most advisable in life is to be sensitive
enough to feel life and its beauty and to appreciate
it, but at the same time to consider that one's soul is
divine, and that all else is foreign to it; that all things
that belong to the earth are foreign to one's soul.

June 14

When I open my eyes to the outer world I feel myself as a drop in the sea; but when I close my eyes and look within, I see the whole universe as a bubble raised in the ocean of my heart.

June 15

The soul does not wither and get worn out, but what it has gathered around it on earth, what it has imagined itself to be, all that it has taken from the lower plane, withers and becomes worn out.

June 16

It is the situation we are in that makes us believe we are this or that. Whatever the soul experiences, that it believes itself to be. If the soul sees the external self as a baby it believes, "I am a baby." If it sees the external self as old it believes, "I am old." If it sees the external self in a palace it believes, "I am rich." If it sees that self in a hut it believes, "I am poor." But in reality it is only, "I am...." When man lives in this limitation he does not know that another part of his being exists, which is much higher, more wonderful, more living, and more exalted.

June 17

Every experience on the physical or astral plane is just a dream before the soul. It is ignorance when it takes this experience to be real.

June 18

It is the path of discipline that leads to the goal of liberty.

June 19

Free will is the mighty power, the God power hidden in man, and it is ignorance that keeps man from his divine heritage.

June 20

The difference between the divine and the human will is like the difference between the trunk of a tree and its branches. As from the boughs other twigs and branches spring, so the will of one powerful individual has branches going through the will of other individuals. So there are the powerful beings, the masters of humanity. Their will is God's will, their word is God's word, and yet they are branches, because the trunk is the will of the Almighty. Whether the branch be large or small, every branch has the same origin and the same root as the stem.

June 21

The soul's unfoldment comes from its own power, which ends in its breaking through the ties of the lower planes. It is free by nature, and looks for freedom during its captivity. All the holy beings of the world have become so by freeing the soul, its freedom being the only object there is in life.

June 22

There are two forces, *kaza* and *kadr*. Kaza is the force that is all-powerful, and kadr is the force of an individual will power. An individual goes on running his hoop as far as his power allows him to, but there comes a wagon that blocks the road, and the hoop cannot go further. It is that wagon that is kaza, the all-powerful, which comes into conflict with the individual power. This idea is so well expressed in the saying, "Man proposes but God disposes."

June 23

In a small affair or in a big affair, first consult yourself and find out if there is any conflict in your own being about anything you want to do. And when you find no conflict there, then feel sure that a path is already made for you. You have but to open your eyes and take a step forward, and the other step will be led by God.

June 24

There is nothing valuable except what we value in life.

June 25

The power that acquires a thing develops the power of holding it; the power that holds a thing develops the power of increasing it; but the power that lets a

thing go loses the power to hold it and at last
becomes too weak ever to acquire it again.

June 26

When you gain a thing from another you may have
to pass it on to another also when the time comes.

June 27

The one who has earned and used what he has
earned has gained. The one who earned and
collected and departed has lost.

June 28

It is the optimist who takes the initiative; the
pessimist follows him.

June 29

Possibility is the nature of God, and impossibility is
the limitation of man.

June 30

Every thought and imagination of a mystic has an
effect. When he thinks of something it may
materialize the week after, or the next month, or
perhaps after many years, but all that a mystic says
or thinks is fulfilled sooner or later.

July 1

While using the inner power, beware. There are taps of water which, once opened, may flood the whole world; and there are volcanoes which, once made to burst, may set fire to the whole universe. Man must not play with the power latent in his soul; he must know toward what end he uses the power and to what extent he is able to control and use the power.

July 2

Some thoughts are like things, like objects; other thoughts are like beings. Some thoughts are like angels by our side, and some are like devils. They are all around us, either helping us towards the accomplishment of the objects before us or drawing us back from those things we wish to accomplish.

July 3

Once one bad thought is created, in the spirit of anger or annoyance, a thousand other spirits are created out of it.

July 4

One aspect of man's being is like a machine, the other aspect of his being is like an engineer.

July 5

The machine part of man's being is dependent upon what is put into it in order to stay in working condition. And there is another machine, a fine mechanism that works as the inner part of this machine, that is finer than its outer part. And that fine part feels atmosphere, feels vibrations, feels pleasures and displeasures. This machine is made for the use of the other part of one's being, which is the engineer.

July 6

On the day when the engineer part of man begins to waken, that day he begins to feel mastery over this machine. He begins to know on that day that this machine was made for him to work it to the best advantage.

July 7

The spirit of limitation is always a hindrance to realizing the spirit of mastery and practicing it. The experience of being powerless is man's ignorance of the power within him.

July 8

How far is man granted the power of mastering his destiny and how far does he stand in this life helpless? The answer is that a soul is born on earth helpless, and out of this helplessness it grows and then learns to help itself. Man has two aspects of being: the servant aspect and the master aspect. When only the servant aspect is nourished and the master aspect is not, then the master aspect of his being longs to be master, and cannot. There is a stage of evolution in which man is the engineer who works with the machines, but the man who has not realized the kingdom of heaven within him is as a machine.

July 9

The sage battles with his own ego; the ordinary man with other people's egos.

July 10

True power is not in trying to gain power; true power is in becoming power. But how to become power? It requires an attempt to make a definite change in oneself, and that change is a kind of struggle with one's false self. When the false self is crucified, then the true self is resurrected. Before the world this crucifixion appears to be lack of power, but in truth all power is attained by this resurrection.

July 11

When a soul arrives at its full bloom, it begins to show the color and spread the fragrance of the divine spirit of God. And once man has arrived at that pitch, he begins to express the manner of God in everything he does. And what is the manner of God? It is the kingly manner which is not known even to kings.

July 12

The real dervish is the king wherever he is. Neither money, a coat, nor life in the world can take away his kingship from him. If he chooses to live in solitude, it is his own affair. If he wishes to be in the crowd, he may just as well be there. Whether a person sits in a remote place in the forest or in a baker's shop, if he is thinking of a high ideal his surroundings cannot touch him. There is no aspect of life that can deprive a mystic of his mystical spirit.

July 13

A king is ever a king, be he crowned with a jewelled crown or clad in a beggar's garb.

July 14

There is no impulse that in its beginning is wrong. It is during the process through which the impulse passes that it becomes right or wrong.

July 15

The discovery of the very least thing is the discovery of the whole of humanity. The whole of humanity has shared in everything that we think new today.

July 16

By learning self-discipline one learns to suppress the outer inclinations in order to make way for the inner inclinations to rise and flourish, which finally culminates in what we call mastery.

July 17

The entire system of the yogis is based upon making themselves acquainted with something their nature revolts against.

July 18

The first thing to do is to get control of the glance. The next is to get control of the feelings. And the third is to get control of the consciousness.

July 19

When a person progresses toward spirituality he must bear in mind that together with his spiritual progress he must strengthen himself against disturbing influences. If not he should know that however much he desires to make progress he will be pulled back against his will by conditions, by circumstances. When he cannot put up with conditions around him he may think that he is a superior person, but in reality the conditions are stronger than he.

July 20

A man who is helpless before his own mind is helpless before everything in the world. Mastery lies not merely in stilling the mind, but in directing it towards whatever point we desire, in allowing it to be active as far as we wish, in using it to fulfil our purpose, in causing it to be still when we want to still it.

July 21

There is yet another aspect of self-discipline, and that is to practice the forgetting of things so that certain thoughts may not get a hold over one's mind, and in the same way to check thoughts of agitation, anger, depression, prejudice, hatred. This gives moral discipline, and by doing so one becomes the master of one's mind.

July 22

A person who expresses an opinion about another readily, a mist is produced by his word before his own eyes; he can see no further than he sees. If he controlled that impulse of expressing his opinion it would be an effort at that moment, but it would

open before him the vision revealing all that he
would wish to know.

July 23

A person who has anger and control is to be
preferred to the person who has neither.

July 24

The first exercise to help the will power to develop
would be to check every act, word, and thought
which we do not wish to occur; to avoid
unintentional actions, speech, and thoughts.

July 25

One must check the wrong impulse: an impulse to
talk back to a person who insults one, an impulse to
pinch a person by saying a word, an impulse to hurt
a person by cutting words, an impulse to find out
the secret of others, an impulse to criticize. All such
undesirable impulses can be mastered. And it is not
that one has mastered them, but one has gained
power over oneself.

July 26

Every impulse is a power in itself, and every time
the will withdraws an impulse, the will is charged
with a new strength and life, which makes the
self-mastered man master of all. The process of
alchemy is to control these expressions without
killing them. There is a difference between

controlling and killing. By controlling, one possesses power without allowing it to express itself; but by killing, one loses it.

July 27

Mastery is greater than seership, because the master both sees and accomplishes.

July 28

Man is tuned by his surroundings and man can tune himself in spite of his surroundings.

July 29

The purpose of life is to attain to mastery; this is the motive of the spirit, and it is through this motive at the back of it that the whole universe is created.

July 30

The path of the master requires self-discipline and will power to make headway through life. He conquers himself; he battles with life; he is at war with destiny; he crusades against all that seems to him wrong.

July 31

If you wish people to obey you, you must learn to obey yourself; if you wish people to believe you, you must learn to believe yourself; if you wish people to respect you, you must learn to respect yourself; if you wish people to trust you, you must learn to trust yourself.

August 1

Do we not see, even in our own limited experience, how things go wrong when we have become weak in will or mind in one affair or another? It is not possible to master the conditions of life until we have learned to control ourselves. Once we have mastery over ourself everything will go right.

August 2

The Yogi says that it is better to leave the world, but the Sufi chooses a life in the world with renunciation. The Sufi has no need to run away from the world, for he has recognized and sees the face of his Beloved, the face of God, everywhere.

August 3

Renunciation is a flight of stairs by which to rise above all things. For all things of this world that man thinks he possesses he does not really possess; in reality he is possessed by them, be it wealth, or property, or a friend, or rank.

August 4

You may be in a situation where you want to accomplish something, and people laugh at you or are apt to criticize you. In that situation, you should be indifferent. But if in order to promote your business you have to see someone to get connections, all this will only succeed according to your interest. If you are indifferent about it, you will defeat your own ends.

August 5

Indifference gives great power. But the whole manifestation is a phenomenon of interest. All this world that man has made, where has it come from? It has come from the power of interest. The whole creation and all that is in it are the product of the Creator's interest. But at the same time the power of indifference is a greater one still, because although motive has a power, yet at the same time motive limits power. Yet it is motive that gives man the power to accomplish things.

August 6

In order to perform his duty man may have to struggle with himself, he may have to go through suffering and pain, he may have to pass many tests and trials. By making many sacrifices and practicing renunciation, he will attain that consciousness that is God-consciousness, in which resides all perfection.

August 7

While the immortal demands the sacrifice of your activity, the mortal demands the sacrifice of your peace.

August 8

It is the nature of life in the world that all the things we become attracted to in time become not only ties but burdens.

August 9

What is made for man, man may hold; he must not be held by it.

August 10

One can love one's friends and yet be detached. The way of those who renounce is to know all things, to admire all things, to get all things, but give all things, and to think that nothing belongs to them and that they own nothing.

August 11

Renounce momentarily precious things for everlasting things. Every step of progress is made by renouncing more personal values for more cosmic ones.

August 12

It is easy to tie a knot of attachment, but it is difficult when we wish to unravel it.

August 13

Sacrifice and renunciation are two things; sacrifice is made by love, renunciation is caused by indifference.

August 14

The ideal is the means, but its breaking is the goal.

August 15

Sometimes by going in pursuit of a thing one gains it; sometimes it is achieved by merely waiting to receive it.

August 16

The great kings of the world very often have been pulled down from their thrones by those who for years bowed and bent and trembled at their command, but the Christlike souls who have washed the feet of the disciples are still held in esteem, and will be honored and loved by humanity forever.

August 17

No one has entrance into the kingdom of God who has not been crucified. Those who are given liberty by Him to act freely, are nailed on the earth, and those who are free to act as they choose on the earth will be nailed in the heavens.

August 18

The bringers of joy have always been the children of sorrow. Out of the shell of the broken heart emerges the newborn soul.

August 19

The heart, like a bell, wants striking, and in the resonance of the heart the purpose of that activity is fulfilled.

August 20

It is not the sore heart that can always become a mirror, it is the etherealized heart that becomes transparent.

August 21

The pain of life is the price paid for the quickening of the heart.

August 22

The real proof of one's progress in the spiritual path can be realized by testing in every situation of life how indifferent one is. There are calls from every side, from all that is good, from all that is beautiful, from all that is kind, from all that is comforting. And when one has shown indifference to all these calls, then one begins to hear calls from one's immediate surroundings. Those are a wish that one's goodness may be appreciated and that one's kindness may be gratefully received, that one's knowledge may be understood by others, one's rank may be recognized, one's piety may be observed by others, one's virtue may be valued, and one's good qualities may find response, one's good actions may bear fruit. The more one makes oneself free from all these calls the more one becomes raised above life.

August 23

The ideal of God is preached in order to make the perfect Being intelligible. However, the limitless God cannot be made intelligible to the limited self unless He is first made limited.

August 24

He is an unbeliever who cannot believe in himself. The trust of someone who trusts another but does not trust himself is profitless. But someone who trusts another because he trusts himself has the real trust, and by this trust in himself he can make his life happy whatever his condition may be.

August 25

Belief is of four kinds. The first kind is a belief accepted because it is believed by all. The second is a belief accepted because it is believed by someone in whom the believer trusts. The third belief is the belief that reason helps one to believe. The fourth belief is conviction, of which one is as sure as if one were an eyewitness.

August 26

There are natures which would be willing to believe a thing if it is for their good, if it comes from someone whom they trust, but for them it is too much trouble to go deeply into the matter. When a person is content with his belief, that is a comfortable state of being, but it is the understanding of the belief that is the ideal.

August 27

It is a certain grade of evolution that enables man to understand a certain belief, and he must not be told what he is incapable of understanding, for then, instead of helping him, it puts him off.

August 28

Every belief and every experience for a wise person is a step of a staircase; when he has taken this step, there is another step for him to take. The steps of the staircase are not made for one to stand there. They are made for one to pass, to go further, because life is progress. The progressive soul can never hold one belief, and must change and go on changing until it arrives at the ultimate truth.

August 29

Today religion remains in the hands of those who have kept it in its outer form, through devotion and loyalty to their ancestors' faith; and those who are, so to speak, grown up in mind and spirit and who want something better, they can find nothing.

August 30

We doubt, and, by that very doubt, that which we fear happens, because it is created by us in the other person's heart.

August 31

The great power that mind has is nothing but the power of faith. People who have done great works have not done them because of their worldly heritage, for instances occur in which people began life without a penny and yet have ended their lives the possessors of millions. They have raised their position themselves. When there is faith there is no thought about whether there are any means of accomplishing the desire that has entered one's mind, or whether there are no means.

September 1

It is natural for man to make God that which he thinks to be best; therefore whether people belong to the same religion or nation or not, each one of them has his own God, depending on the way he looks upon Him. Each person's God is as he looks upon Him; and if one says that there are as many Gods as there are people in the world, that is also true.

September 2

When the question of faith arises, the orthodox always think that it is their religion which is being spoken of. To have faith in a religion, in the priests or clergy, in a certain dogma, ceremony, principle, or in a certain form of teaching, that is what is usually understood by the word faith. The mystic does not mean by faith a belief in a certain religion or dogma or ceremony or book or teacher: he means trust, a trust even in the absence of reason.

September 3

There are many religions existing today called *a* religion, but what is needed today is *the* religion. Must this be a new religion? If it were to be a new religion it could not be called *the* religion. *The* religion is that religion which one can see by rising above sects and differences which divide men. I do not mean that all the religions are not religion; they are the notes, but there is the music, and that music is *the* religion.

September 4

The God of the monotheist is within him, made by his mind, though it is only the form of God that he makes; the spirit is always the same, hidden behind him.

September 5

The words of the Prophet of Islam may be quoted, where he says, "Every soul has its own religion," which means that every soul has a certain direction which it has chosen. This goal is a certain ideal that depends on the soul's evolution.

September 6

In order to attain to God-consciousness the first condition is to make God a reality, so that He is no longer only an imagination.

September 7

When wealth was esteemed, the message was delivered by King Solomon; when beauty was worshipped, Joseph, the most handsome, gave the message; when music was regarded as celestial, David gave his message in song; when there was curiosity about miracles, Moses brought his message; when sacrifice was highly esteemed, Abraham gave the message; when heredity was recognized, Christ gave his message as the son of God; and when democracy was necessary, Muhammmad gave his message as the servant of God, one like all and among all.

September 8

The followers of each form of the message profess devotion to their lord and master, by whatever name he had in the past, but they do not necessarily know the master. What they know is the name and the life of the master that has come down to them in history or tradition; but beyond that they know very little about him. If the same one came in another form, in a garb adapted to another age, would they know him or accept him?

September 9

In the outer sense of the word religion is a form given to the worship of God, and a law given to a community to help it to live harmoniously. In the

inner sense of the word, religion means a staircase
made for the soul to climb and reach that plane
where truth is realized.

September 10

Did Jesus Christ come to form an exclusive
community called Christianity, or Buddha to found
a creed called Buddhism? Was it Muhammad's ideal
to form a community called Muhammadan? On the
contrary, the Prophet warned his disciples that they
should not attach his name to his message, but that
it should be called Islam, the Message of Peace.

September 11

Energy cannot exist without the energetic, to whom
energy belongs. Might cannot exist without the
mighty one, whose attribute it is. Intelligence cannot
exist without the intelligent one, to whom that
intelligence belongs.

September 12

God is a being who includes everyone and all
things, and therefore there is nothing with which
one can compare this Being.

September 13

There is no way of getting proof of God's existence
except by becoming acquainted with oneself, by
experiencing the phenomena that are within one.

September 14

It is owing to our limitation that we cannot see the whole being of God.

September 15

It is the consciousness of the God who is never absent that gives that illumination, those riches, that strength, that calm and peace to the soul for which the soul has taken the journey through this world of limitations. Experiencing life through the form of man it accomplishes its purpose, and the wish with which it started from heaven is fulfilled on earth. It is through man that God completes His creation.

September 16

Man is not made by God as the wood is cut by the carpenter, for the carpenter and the wood are different, while God and man are the same. He creates of Himself; consequently His manifestation is also God. Man is made of the substance of God; man is in God, and all that is in God is in man.

September 17

One person thinks that there is a God, and the other sees God

September 18

At present there exists in the world only a belief in God; God exists in imagination, in the ideal. It is such a soul which has touched divine perfection that brings to the earth a living God, who without him would remain only in the heavens.

September 19

No doubt it would be a great mistake to say that God is only a personality, but it is a still greater mistake when man denies the personality of God.

September 20

Only that part of God is intelligible which man makes. Man makes it in the form of man or out of the attributes that seem to him good in man.

September 21

No sooner is the God ideal brought to life than the worshipper of God turns into truth.

September 22

Some think that if all is God then God cannot be a person; but to this it may be answered that though the seed does not show the flower in it, yet the seed culminates in a flower, and therefore the flower has already existed in the seed.

September 23

The man who sees God in one object only and not in all things and beings, it is he who is the idolater.

September 24

A Buddhist statue in India has Indian features, in China has Chinese features, and in Japan has Japanese features. This is natural. When man pictures angels he draw them like human beings; he only adds wings to them. Man cannot imagine God's personality as being different from man's personality; that is why he attaches to God his ideal of the perfect man.

September 25

The heart of man, as Sufis say, is a mirror. All that is reflected in this mirror is projected upon other mirrors. When man has doubt in his heart, that doubt is reflected upon every heart with which he comes in contact; when he has faith, that faith is reflected in every heart.

September 26

Blessed is he who sees the star of his soul as the light that is seen in the port from the sea.

September 27

God-realized ones bring to the world the living
God.

September 28

If there is any sign of God to be seen, it is in the
God-conscious one, and it is the fullness of
God-consciousness that makes a prophetic soul.

September 29

The prophetic soul must of necessity rise so high
that it can hear the voice of God, and at the same
time it must bend so low that it can hear the softest
whisper of the beings on earth.

September 30

How difficult it is to translate fully the poetry of one
language into the poetry of another. Yet it is only
interpreting the ideas of one part of the earth to the
people of another part of the same earth. How much
more difficult, then, it must be to translate or to
interpret the ideas of the divine world to the human
world.

October 1

It was necessary, so to speak, that God should walk on earth in the physical body.

October 2

Some object to Christ being called divine, but if divinity is not sought in man, then in what shall we seek for God? And if on the other hand someone else calls Christ man, he only raises the standard of man to the highest point.

October 3

All the teachers who came before taught for whatever community or group of people they were born, and prophesied the coming of the next teacher, foreseeing the possibility and the necessity of the continuation of the message until its fulfillment.

October 4

There is a stage at which, by touching a particular phase of existence, one feels raised above the limitations of life and given that power and peace and freedom, that light and life, which belong to the source of all beings. In that moment of supreme exaltation one is not only united with the source of all beings, but dissolved in it, for the source is one's self. It is just like touching the presence of God, when one's consciousness has become so light and so liberated and free that it can raise itself and dive and touch the depths of one's being.

October 5

There is a time in life when a passion is awakened in the soul that gives the soul a longing for the unattainable, and if the soul does not take that direction, then it certainly misses something in life for which it has an innate longing and in which lies its ultimate satisfaction.

October 6

There comes a time in one's evolution when every touch of beauty moves the heart to tears, and it is at that time that the Beloved of heaven is brought on earth.

October 7

True exaltation of the spirit resides in the fact that it has come to earth and has realized there its spiritual existence.

October 8

A man who has gone through all experiences and has held his spirit high, not allowing it to be stained, such a man may be said to be pure-minded. The person who could be called pure because he had no knowledge of either good or evil would in reality be merely a simpleton. To go through all that takes away the original purity and yet to rise above everything that seeks to overwhelm it and drag it down, that is spirituality: the light of the spirit held high and burning clear and pure.

October 9

By following a certain principle in life one gains a power that comes as an intoxication.

October 10

When the deeper side of man's nature is touched, what is hidden in it manifests on the surface.

October 11

Exaltation comes by touching the reason of reasons and by realizing the essence of wisdom, by feeling the profound depth of one's heart, by widening one's outlook on life, by broadening one's conception, by deepening one's sympathies. A further cause of exaltation comes when we have asked forgiveness and humbled ourselves before someone towards whom we were inconsiderate. We

have humbled our pride then. Or when we have felt
a deep gratitude to someone who had done
something for us, when we have felt love, sympathy,
devotion that seems endless and that seems so great
that our heart cannot accommodate it, when we
have felt so much pity for someone that we have
forgotten ourselves, when we have found a
profound happiness in rendering a humble service
to someone in need, when we have said a prayer
that has come from the bottom of our heart, when
we have realized our own limitation and smallness
in comparison with the greatness of God. All these
experiences lift man up.

October 12

Spiritual magnetism is produced in man when at
the command of his own will he becomes absorbed
in the abstract, making his senses controlled and
inactive, enjoying the undertone of the universe on
which all the music of the universe is based. This
state of ecstasy then attracts, much like an electric
current, all who may come in contact with him,
either consciously or unconsciously. It is of this
magnetism that Christ said to the fishermen, "Come
hither; I will make you the fishers of men."

October 13

The presence of the mystic becomes as wine for
everyone who comes into his presence.

October 14

What the Sufi calls wine is the pleasure he derives
when he sees what activates all the different lives. It
is like drinking wine. One will always find that the
most evolved sages can be amused. It is the tickling
of the mind that produces humor.

October 15

One can know the grade of a person's evolution by
knowing what causes him to laugh and what causes
him to cry. Every person is tuned to a certain pitch,
and that which causes a person to laugh or weep
must be in some way in accordance with his pitch.

October 16

There are many ideas that intoxicate man; many
feelings act upon the soul as wine; but there is no
stronger wine than selflessness.

October 17

Very often people think that sorrow or pain is the
sign of spirituality. Yes, in many cases sorrow or
pain becomes a process that leads to attaining
spirituality quickly, but for that one need not afflict
oneself with sorrow or pain, for life has enough
sorrow or pain.

October 18

As fire can cook food or burn it, so also does pain affect the human heart.

October 19

The spirit of feeling is lost when a sentiment is expressed in words. Do you think a person who really loves need say, "I love you"? No, the word love cannot express his feeling: it is too small in comparison to what love means to him who truly loves. Yes, there is a beauty in words, as there is beauty in flowers. But the flowers may be called the angels of the earth. They live only in heaven: on earth they appear for a moment and fade away. The feelings are like angels. The one who lives in his feelings lives in heaven, and when he puts them into words he drops down on the earth. And however beautiful his imagination and his choice of words, he turns angels into flowers.

October 20

Silence is taught in every school of the inner cult.

October 21

I will soar higher than the highest heaven,
I will dive deeper than the depths of the ocean,
I will reach further than the wide horizon,
I will enter within my innermost being.

You know me but little, O ever-changing life,

I will live in that sphere where death cannot reach.

I will raise my head high before you will turn your
back to me,

I will close my lips before you will close the doors of
your heart,

I will dry my tears before you will not respond to
my sigh,

I will fly to the heavens, O world of illusion, before
you will throw me down on the earth.

October 22

If this world is the work of a Creator, it has been
created so that He might experience external life.
Inasmuch as it is necessary for the knowing aspect
of life, or the soul, to return at length to its original
state of being, even so it is necessary for it to
experience first of all the life it created for the very
reason that it might know.

October 23

The expression of intense affection towards the
opposite sex brings the whole being to the surface.
Consciousness, which in other experiences becomes
but partially external, remaining mostly within, is
brought entirely to the surface by sex passion alone.
It is because of this that spiritually-minded people
have abstained from sex passion and religious
people have considered it degrading.

October 24

It is the spirit that possesses the sexes, to draw them together for its own purpose of manifestation. And therefore many religions and philosophies have considered the sex relationship the most sacred of all, since it is thus that the spirit manifests itself. And for the same reason the sex relationship may become the most sinful of all, if this purpose of the spirit is lost to view. While every expression of life — speech, laughter, tears — robs man of some part of his fund of energy, it is sex passion that makes the greatest demand of all. Therefore the ideal of celibacy was presented, so that man might the better preserve his energy to pursue with singleness of vision that final goal of spiritual attainment.

October 25

Passion is life itself; it is energy taking substantial form and expressing itself through different channels and outlets.

October 26

Man's life can never be complete without woman, and this is the error that lies at the root of the ideal of celibacy.

October 27

The furthest stage in development is the *nafs-e salima*, in which man's consciousness is removed to an abstract plane. In the heart of a man at this point of evolution, love is raised from admiration to worship. His love is part of his being, and his passion, which is never expressed except in the intensity of love, may be compared to the alighting of a bird on earth to pick up a grain of corn. He may become gradually etherealized above every material object. Having reached this point he is truly justified if he should strike the path of celibacy.

October 28

The secret of woman's charm is her modesty; the mystery of man's power is his pride.

October 29

Man has always guarded the treasures that he values most in all sorts of covering, and since that which man can love most is woman, he has often ignorantly tried to guard her in the same way as all things of value and importance. She has therefore been considered in the East as one enshrined and worthy to be guarded from the strife of the world which man, more roughly made, can more easily bear.

October 30

Every soul has its domain in life, consisting of all it possesses and of all who belong to it. This domain is as wide as the width of the soul's influence; it is, so to speak, a mechanism that works by the thought power of each individual soul.

October 31

Man's every passion, emotion, impulse, or action that robs the soul of its power has its reaction not only upon the man but upon the domain.

November 1

One thing is that a person asks himself how all he sees affects him and what is his reaction to it all; how does his spirit react to the objects or the conditions he encounters, to the sounds he hears, to the words that people speak to him? And the second thing is to see what effect he himself has on others, conditions, and individuals when he comes in contact with them.

November 2

When we judge others, we are certainly judging the Artist who has created them.

November 3

When we see the reason behind every fault that appears to us in anyone we meet in our life, we become more tolerant, we become more forgiving.

November 4

What is the duty of real brothers and sisters? To cover the faults of one another.

November 5

Receiving kindness from others only makes the recipient expect more. He keeps saying, "He is doing this for his own benefit; he is not considering me; he is blaming me; he did not help me; he did not deal fairly with me." His life becomes full of grudges because he expects from everybody all the good that he wants, and he does not know that he ought to have it all in himself, that he should become independent. Therein lies the secret of character.

November 6

Nature is born, character is built, and personality is developed.

November 7

When one rises morally above the tendency to devote one's time and thought to other people's affairs that do not concern one in any way — speaking about them, forming opinions about people — when all this is given up, then a person becomes entitled to spiritual attainment.

November 8

We occupy only as much horizon as we are conscious of. Every individual has his own world, and the world of one individual is as tiny as a grain of lentil, and that of another as large as the whole world.

November 9

There is no piece of consciousness cut out for man, but man occupies a certain horizon, as far as he can expand; for him the absolute can be his consciousness. Therefore on the outside he is individual, but in reality one cannot say what he is.

November 10

Spirituality is not a certain knowledge, spirituality is the expansion of consciousness. The wider the consciousness expands, the greater is one's spiritual vision. And when once the consciousness expands so much that it embraces the whole universe, it is that which is called divine perfection.

November 11

There are two directions or dimensions in which to expand. The one is the outward, the other the inner dimension.

November 12

If one is able to expand oneself to the consciousness of another person, one's consciousness becomes as large as two persons'. And so it can become as large as a thousand persons' when one accustoms oneself to try and see what others think. It is the understanding of two points of view, the opposite points of view, that gives a fuller insight into life. The "I" and "you" only remain as long as we see ourselves, but when we rise above them or beyond them, the thought brings us nearer and nearer to God in that consciousness in which we all unite.

November 13

This space of three dimensions is reflected by the space that is in the inner dimension. The inner dimension is different: it does not belong to the objective world, but what exists in the inner dimension is also reflected in three-dimensional space. So in reality what the mystic sees in space is something that is within. When a mystic closes his eyes he sees it within, but when he opens his eyes he sees it before him.

November 14

The Sufi practices that process through which he is able to touch that part of life in himself that is not subject to death.

November 15

Tuning ourselves to the infinite is achieved by the way of silence, by the way of meditation, by the way of thinking of something that is beyond and above all things of this mortal world; by giving some moments of our life to the thought of getting in tune with that which is the source and goal of all of us.

November 16

Only self-realization can give man full independence. The world in which man lives like a drop in the sea then becomes a drop in the ocean of his heart.

November 17

My smallest work in the inner plane is worth more than all I do in the outer world.

November 18

The sun neither rises nor sets; it is our conception. When the earth turns its back to the sun, it is night; when the earth turns its face to the sun, it is day.

November 19

The lesson we learn from the development of our insight is not to become excited by any influence that tries to bring us out of rhythm, but to stay in rhythm under all conditions of life.

November 20

As the eyes cannot see themselves, so it is with the soul: it is sight itself, and therefore it sees all. The moment it closes its eyes to all it sees, its own light makes it manifest to its own view. It is for this reason that people take the path of meditation.

November 21

Each atom of this universe, conscious of its sickness, procures for itself from within or without a means for its restoration.

November 22

By being conscious of one's magnetism one develops it.

November 23

The physical and mental faculties should be opened in such a way that the electric vibrations in the various planes of existence may be enabled to operate. Physical vibrations depend upon the purity and energy of the body, and they can be projected through the finer organs, such as the palms of the hands, the tips of the fingers, the soles of the feet, the tongue, the cheek, the forehead, the ear, the lips, nose, and eyes. The finest of all these is the eye.

November 24

Action develops magnetism, but repose controls it. That is why very active people always develop their magnetism, but without being able to hold it. It is like earning money from one side, spending it on the other, and always being without.

November 25

The presence of souls who have awakened is itself a magnetism; it draws people walking on the earth and it draws souls that are not seen on the earth.

November 26

In old age, neither freshness nor development of the body remains the same, nor does the power of mind. If then there is any attraction, it is only the illumination of the soul that has a great magnetic influence over man's surroundings.

November 27

You will find that numberless people who are most highly qualified do not make their way through life because of lack of magnetism.

November 28

A selfless person tends to scatter the atoms of the astral and auric substance of his being, causing it to radiate, while the more selfish person condenses the atoms within the confines of his body.
Consequently, the auras of more selfless people shine more brightly.

November 29

The soul on its journey onward strikes a plane where it exclaims, "I am the truth!" There are two things: knowing and being. It is easy to know truth, but most difficult to be truth. It is not in knowing truth that life's purpose is accomplished: life's purpose is accomplished in being truth.

November 30

Among the seekers after truth, we find only one who is courageous enough to look at the immensity of truth.

December 1

All situations of life are tests to bring out the real and the false.

December 2

When a person does not listen to us, we must know that it is because we ourselves do not believe.

December 3

The voice of the insincere person comes from the surface and reaches the ears. The voice of the sincere person comes from the depth and goes to the depth.

December 4

Faithfulness has a fragrance that is perceptible in the atmosphere of the faithful.

December 5

Fact is intelligible, but truth is beyond comprehension, for truth is unlimited.

December 6

There are many who do not mind if they hurt anyone as long as they think they have told the truth. There is, however, a difference between fact and truth. Fact is that which can be spoken of; truth is that which cannot be put into words.

December 7

The bare truth alone is not sufficient; truth must be made into wisdom. And what is wisdom? Wisdom is the robe of truth.

December 8

Beyond goodness is trueness, which is a divine quality.

December 9

The moment a person becomes straightforward, a straight way opens before him.

December 10

When a being becomes truth, he reads into the hearts of all beings like an open book. Then a person begins to communicate with all things and all beings. Wherever his glance falls — on nature, on characters — he reads their history, he sees their future. He sees the cause behind the faults people have. While an ordinary person can see the action of another, the seer can see the reason of the action also, and if his sight is still keener, he can see the reason of the person. He knows why an event comes, whence it comes, what is behind it, what is the cause of it, and behind the seeming cause what is the hidden cause; and if he wished to trace the cause behind the cause he could trace back to the primal cause, for the inner life is lived by living with the primal cause, by being in unity with the primal cause.

December 11

In man is awakened that spirit by which the whole universe was created.

December 12

Man is a miniature of Brahma, the Creator. If man were aware of his creativity he would create as he wished, and would make a world of his own. This is the work of the masters, who grow to become, with their spiritual advancement, creators of their own world.

December 13

In man the Creator has, so to speak, completed nature, yet the creative faculty is still working through man, and thus art is the ultimate step in creation. What the Creator had left undone, He has finished through the artist.

December 14

The Sufi sees both the Creator and the creation in man. The limited part of man's being is the creation, and the innermost part of his being is the Creator.

December 15

As the whole of nature is made by God, so the nature of each individual is made by himself.

December 16

Man can produce out of his thought Satan, an angel, or a devil, and he can produce out of his thought God. When he comes to the realization that all is from one source and all is developing to one goal, then he begins to see that that source is God.

December 17

All things in life are materials for wisdom to work with. All that is in our mind and body has a certain use, and by knowing to what advantage it must be utilized, all the property of the body and the mind can very well be used to the best advantage. All feelings, such as attachment, detachment, passion, anger, grief, hilarity, fear, and bewilderment, have their use in our lives, and by each of the above-mentioned feelings we can be profited if we know their mystery. By all thoughts and imaginations and by all faculties of mind, such as will, memory, thought, reason, and the ego, we can bring out desirable products.

December 18

The mind is a magic shell in which a design is made by the imagination, and the same imagination is materialized on the surface.

December 19

The unconscious mind is a storehouse in which thoughts and impressions live. Imagine a person going through a large room where there are all kinds of things exhibited, and yet there is no light except a searchlight in his own hand.

December 20

There is a storehouse of all knowledge in the universal mind. If you can touch it, all the knowledge that is there in amplitude will be poured out to you with perfect ease. For this the doors of memory should be laid open. Divine mind is the stream of the fountain, and each individual mind is just like a drop. Man shows from the beginning of his life on earth signs of having known things that he had never been taught.

December 21

Every imagination that arises in the mind through the day and night has its effect on one's own life and on the life of another.

December 22

When one has imagined something, that imagination is created, and what is once created exists.

December 23

The lines that the will has made on the mind are the directions in which the imagination unconsciously travels.

December 24

It is not necessary to change the notes of the piano; what is necessary is to know how to create harmony among the different notes.

December 25

One cannot teach *akhlak-e Allah*, the divine manner. It comes when the heart is focused on God, and then all that is in God becomes manifest in man. When this realization comes, one cannot speak anymore of the God within. As soon as God is realized, God does not remain within.

December 26

There are ages of aristocracy and there are ages of democracy of all kinds, not only in regard to government but also in regard to religion. There is no doubt that the aristocratic form of religion has been misused. This happens when the religious authority turns religion into a means, an instrument to keep the people under a certain law for worldly purposes. Then naturally that aristocracy breaks down and there comes a time of democracy. And it is necessary that religious democracy should come, because it is in religious democracy that fulfillment of the religious ideal lies. Religious democracy means that no one should ever think that he is human while someone else is divine and that God is in heaven, unattainable, imperceptible, and far away from his soul. He must realize that divinity is in his soul, that God is within him, that his soul can expand because he is not different from God, nor is God different from him. Only the danger of democracy is when it comes too soon, before a person is ripe, then it brings disaster; for man's natural progress is to follow his highest ideal, but when he is blinded by the spirit of democracy he becomes so agitated that he wishes to break that ideal. He comes down instead of going up. The main purpose of life is to ennoble our soul.

December 27

I have not come to teach you that which you know not; I have come to deepen in you that wisdom which is yours already.

December 28

We shall work together, we shall stand hand in hand to do service to humanity. We do not want any claims, we do not want to say, "I am this," or "I am that."

December 29

What is needed is some capable workers who would forget themselves and consider nothing too great a sacrifice in order to work for God and humanity.

December 30

We all have our part to perform in this Message. Our hearts are as one heart, one heart that is offered to God, the perfection of love, of harmony, of beauty, that this heart may become His shrine, and the need of the living God in the world today may be answered.

December 31

One reaches a stage where it is no longer the singer who sings the song, but the song sings the singer.

Hazrat Inayat Khan, founder of the Sufi Order in the West, was born in India in 1882. A master of classical Indian music by the age of twenty, he relinquished a brilliant career to devote himself to the spiritual path. In 1920, acting upon the guidance of his teacher, he became one of the first teachers of the Sufi tradition in the West. For a decade and a half he travelled throughout Europe and the United States, giving lectures and guiding an ever-growing group of seekers. In 1926, he returned to India, where he died the following year.

A catalogue of books relating to Sufism may be obtained from the publisher by writing to:

Omega Publications, Inc.

RD 1 Box 1030E

New Lebanon, NY 12125